SAVE OUR EARTH!
Climate Action Explained

DECREASING SPACE JUNK

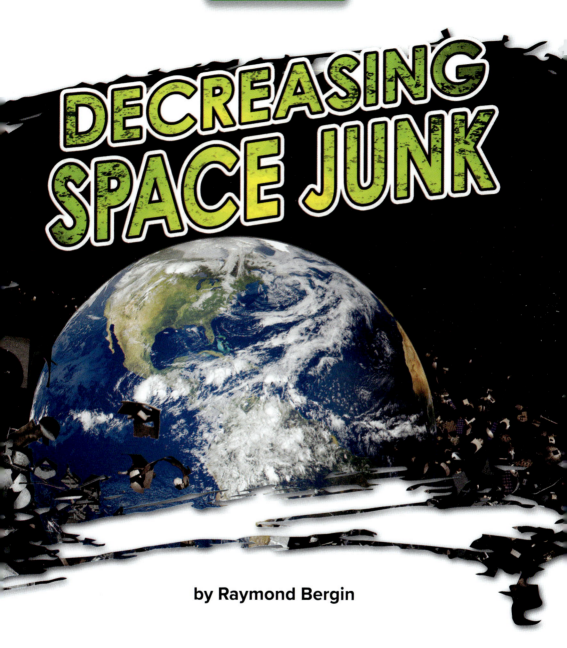

by Raymond Bergin

BEARPORT
PUBLISHING

Minneapolis, Minnesota

Credits
Cover and title page, © 24K-Production/iStock and © Dotted Yeti/Shutterstock; 4–5, © Vadimsadovski/Adobe Stock; 6, © History and Art Collection/Alamy Stock Photo; 7, © JPL/Caltech/NASA; 8–9, © Johnson Space Center/NASA; 10, © Gunnar Lindstrom/Associated Press; 11, © Anadolu/Getty Images; 12–13, © ESA/ID&Sense/ONiRiXEL; 14–15, © Serena Auñón–Chancellor/NASA; 17, © JPL/NASA; 18–19, © Joel Kowsky/NASA; 20–21, © Olexandr/Adobe Stock and © Nada Sertic/Adobe Stock and © Matthew Fox/David Williams Rogers/Hang Woon Lee; 23, © Astroscale/Wikipedia; 24–25, © S. Corvaja/ESA; 26–27, © anatoliy gleb/Adobe Stock; 28, © Kris Wiktor/Adobe Stock; 29TL, © Antonioguillem/Adobe Stock; 29UML, © Tupungato/Shutterstock; 29ML, © Martin Shields/Alamy Stock Photo; 29BML, © Nimito/iStock; 29BL, © fizkes/iStock

Bearport Publishing Company Product Development Team
Publisher: Jen Jenson; Director of Product Development: Spencer Brinker; Managing Editor: Allison Juda; Editor: Cole Nelson; Associate Editor: Tiana Tran; Production Editor: Naomi Reich; Designer: Kim Jones; Designer: Kayla Eggert; Designer: Steve Scheluchin; Production Specialist: Owen Hamlin

Statement on Usage of Generative Artificial Intelligence
Bearport Publishing remains committed to publishing high-quality nonfiction books. Therefore, we restrict the use of generative AI to ensure accuracy of all text and visual components pertaining to a book's subject. See BearportPublishing.com for details.

Library of Congress Cataloging-in-Publication Data is available at www.loc.gov or upon request from the publisher.

ISBN: 979-8-89577-054-2 (hardcover)
ISBN: 979-8-89577-171-6 (ebook)

Copyright © 2026 Bearport Publishing Company. All rights reserved. No part of this publication may be reproduced in whole or in part, stored in any retrieval system, or transmitted in any form or by any means, electronic, mechanical, photocopying, recording, or otherwise, without written permission from the publisher. Bearport Publishing is a division of FlutterBee Education Group.

For more information, write to Bearport Publishing, 3500 American Blvd W, Suite 150, Bloomington, MN 55431.

Contents

Trashing Space........................... 4
Getting Off the Ground.................. 6
Making a Mess 8
Heads Up!.............................. 10
Fast and Furious 12
Path of Destruction 14
Tracking the Trash: Orbital Debris
    Program 16
Launch, Return, Repeat: Falcon 9 18
Laser Lab: SSORL 20
Taking Out the Trash: Astroscale 22
Recycling in Space! Zero Debris ESA 24
Let's Clean Up This Mess!................ 26

Part of the Space Junk Solution!........... 28
Glossary............................... 30
Read More............................. 31
Learn More Online 31
Index.................................. 32
About the Author 32

Trashing Space

Our landfills overflow with garbage, and there is litter everywhere. We've made a real mess of Earth! But we haven't stopped there. People have also been trashing space. High above us, space is crowded with human-made objects that are no longer in use. Dead **satellites**, rocket parts, and pieces of scrap metal circle in the upper **atmosphere** above our planet. It's so cluttered that active satellites and even the International Space Station (ISS) are in danger of devastating collisions. What on Earth is going on high above us?

There is almost 10,000 tons (9,000 t) of **debris** in space around our planet. Most of it is within 1,200 miles (2,000 km) of Earth's surface.

Getting Off the Ground

Humans have long looked up at the night sky in wonder. Yet for a long time, we did not have the technology to explore beyond our planet.

That changed in 1957 when the Soviet Union launched a rocket that put the satellite Sputnik 1 into space. This satellite was sent into an **orbit**, or a circular path, around Earth. In the years since, we have been sending things and even people to space much more frequently. Today, more than 2,500 objects—including satellites, **probes**, and crewed spacecraft—are launched into space every year.

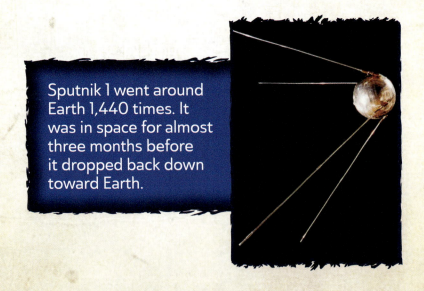

Sputnik 1 went around Earth 1,440 times. It was in space for almost three months before it dropped back down toward Earth.

Satellites can be used to take pictures and gather information. They also help provide internet access as well as send and receive TV, radio, and phone signals.

Making a Mess

Every time a rocket heads into space, it inevitably litters the atmosphere with space junk. This is any piece of human-made debris left in space. All this junk orbits in the farthest parts of the atmosphere around Earth. It can range in size from tiny flecks of paint to **astronaut** tools, dead satellites, or even **discarded** sections of rockets. Currently, there are about 34,000 pieces of space junk larger than 4 inches (10 cm) and hundreds of millions of pieces smaller than that.

> Astronauts have left more than 500,000 pounds (227,000 kg) of trash on the moon. This includes family photos, golf balls, and flags. There are also bags of poop, human ashes, and even vehicles!

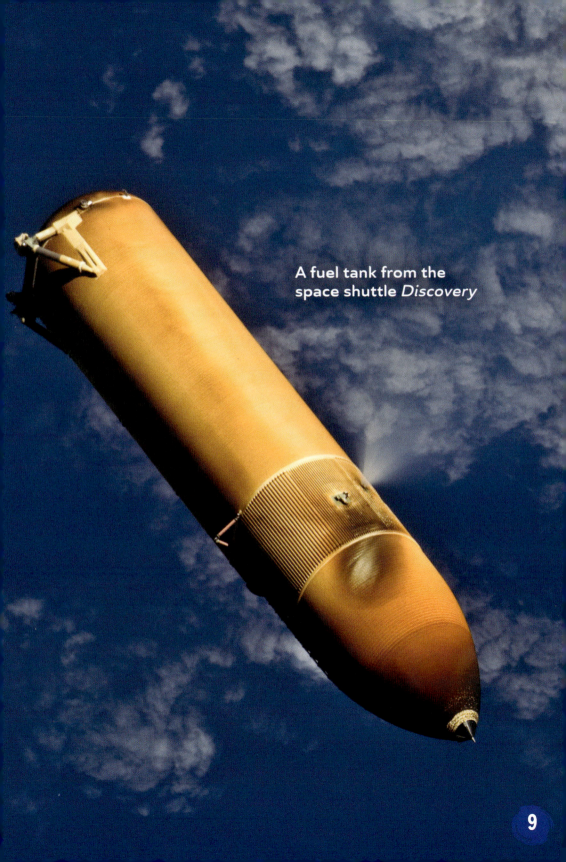

A fuel tank from the space shuttle *Discovery*

Heads Up!

Over time, space junk eventually slows down. It then drops out of orbit and falls back to Earth. Most large satellites are **maneuvered** into place over the ocean before they begin to fall out of orbit. Many larger objects burn up as they travel toward Earth, but careful positioning ensures any pieces that survive reentry will not hit **populated** areas.

Over the last 50 years, an average of 1 piece of space trash has fallen back toward the planet every day. Some of the larger pieces of debris have reached Earth's surface. And the more we put into space, the more we risk danger from pieces falling back down.

Researchers estimate there is a one-in-ten chance of someone being killed by falling space debris before 2032.

Because 70 percent of the planet is covered in ocean, most space debris falls into water. However, in December 2024, a 1,100-lb. (500-kg) piece of space junk landed in Mukuku, Kenya.

Fast and Furious

Even while it's still in the atmosphere, space junk can do some serious damage. Pieces of orbiting debris can travel at 18,000 miles per hour (29,000 kph). That's about seven times faster than a bullet! Most of this debris is metallic and jagged. When it collides with spacecraft, satellites, or other debris, the impact breaks both objects apart and makes more debris. This additional space junk then creates even more collisions—and more space junk. It's a dangerous chain reaction.

> In 2009, a dead Russian satellite collided with an active American communications satellite. The impact created about 2,000 pieces of debris larger than a softball and countless smaller fragments.

Path of Destruction

Along with the hundreds of millions of pieces of junk speeding around in space, about 10,000 active satellites are orbiting our planet. This means the chances of collisions are increasing.

> Several companies are focusing on increasing worldwide internet coverage. This could result in adding as many as 50,000 more satellites into orbit, greatly increasing the odds of collisions.

If active satellites are hit by debris, everyday life on Earth could be impacted. Our TV, phone, and internet systems may go down. If the ISS suffered a large impact, it could be severely damaged or even destroyed. The lives of the astronauts on board would be threatened.

A series of small satellites being deployed

Tracking the Trash
Orbital Debris Program

People are springing into action to avoid catastrophic impacts on—and far above—Earth. The United States space agency, NASA, considers space junk as it plans space missions. Its Orbital Debris Program (ODP) uses **radar** and telescopes to identify objects that are 4 in. (10 cm) or longer. It then tracks this debris in order to select the safest, clearest paths for spacecraft. This trash-tracking information is also used to direct satellites and the ISS away from dangerous oncoming debris.

> There are hundreds of millions of pieces of space debris that are too small to track. So, ODP also designs impact-resistant shielding for NASA spacecraft. These shields break debris into harmless space dust.

This Goldstone antenna can use radar to find space junk.

Launch, Return, Repeat
Falcon 9

About 10 percent of all space junk comes from used rockets. Each of these huge pieces weighs more than 20,000 lb. (9,000 kg) and often contains explosive fuel. The risk of fiery collisions involving this debris worries scientists and mission controllers.

To eliminate this danger, space technology company SpaceX has developed reusable rockets. Once these rockets deliver spacecraft into orbit, they return to Earth. The rockets are then **refurbished** and used again. The reusable rockets leave almost no debris behind.

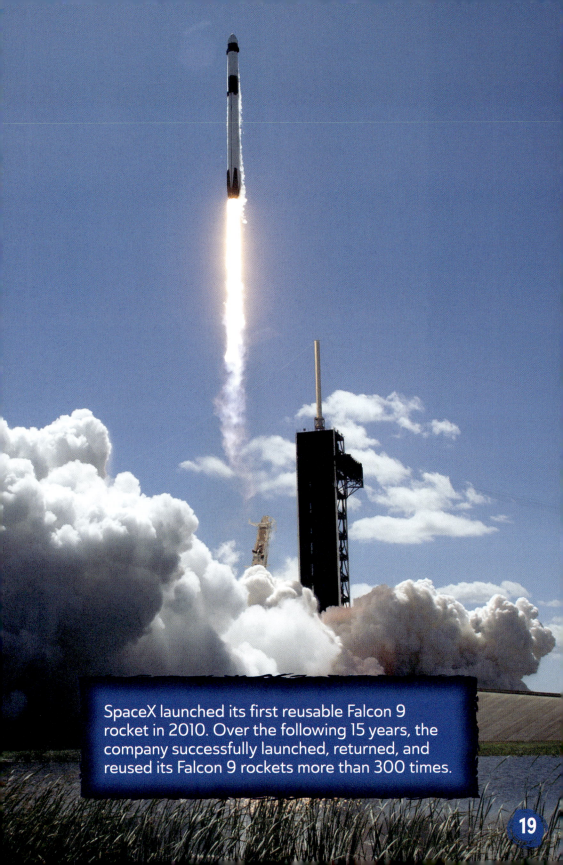

SpaceX launched its first reusable Falcon 9 rocket in 2010. Over the following 15 years, the company successfully launched, returned, and reused its Falcon 9 rockets more than 300 times.

Laser Lab
SSORL

Sometimes, the easiest way to avoid collisions is to simply push **obstacles** out of the way. High-tech **lasers** will soon be doing just that to space junk.

SSORL's lasers are specially designed to **vaporize** a small part of the targeted object. This pushes the remaining material safely off course without breaking it into more pieces.

— Path of satellite-mounted laser

▪▪▪▪▪ Path of object with collision course

— Path that steers clear of collision

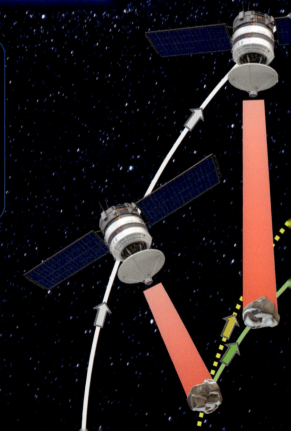

Space Systems Operations Research Laboratory (SSORL) at West Virginia University is developing satellite-mounted lasers that will be able to push aside even tiny pieces of space debris. When this junk is on a collision course with an important object—such as a satellite or the ISS—the laser beams will nudge the space junk into a different orbit. That way, the two objects will not cross paths.

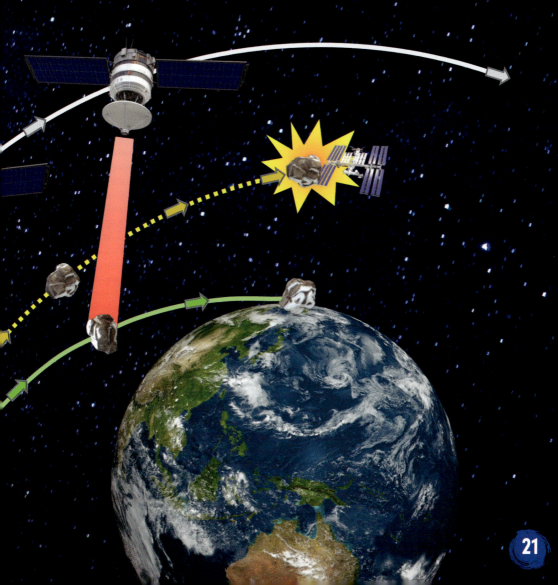

Taking Out the Trash
Astroscale

To really clean up space, we must do more than simply push space junk around. We have to remove it!

A company named Astroscale is developing space garbage trucks that remove dead satellites from orbit. It calls them end-of-life-services-by-Astroscale (ELSA) space-cleaning vehicles. ELSA vehicles will be equipped with magnets that can attract dead satellites. Once the old satellites are captured, the space-cleaning vehicles will drag them out of orbit toward Earth's lower atmosphere. Both craft can then be carefully positioned to safely burn up over the ocean.

> The European Space Agency (ESA) has its own plan for cleaning up space junk. It is testing a spacecraft with a four-armed claw that can capture washing-machine-sized pieces of debris.

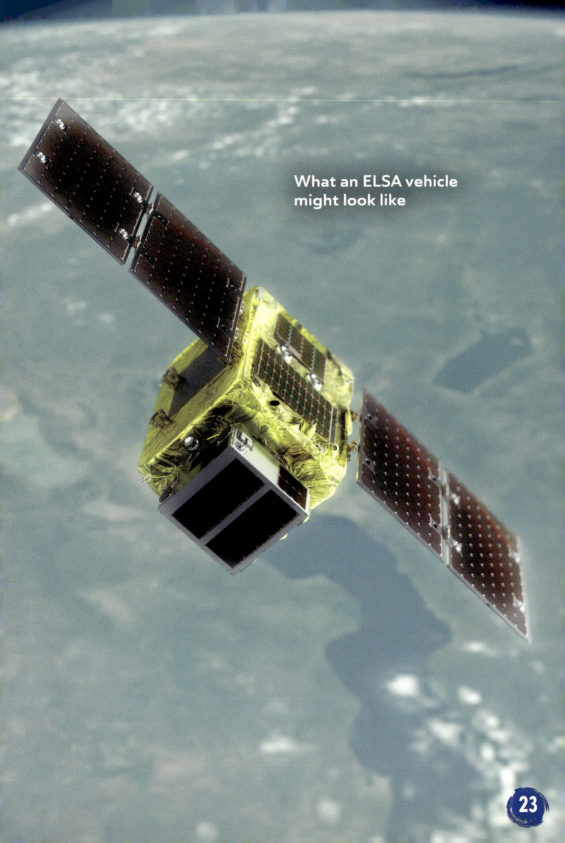

What an ELSA vehicle might look like

Recycling in Space!
Zero Debris ESA

The ESA is working to recycle space junk... while in space! The agency plans to capture debris and bring it to manufacturing and assembly stations in orbit around Earth. The captured material could then be used to build and repair spacecraft, satellites, and even space stations. Fuel collected from dead satellites and spent rockets could be used for active spacecraft. By 2050, ESA hopes to recycle, repurpose, reuse, or refurbish every piece of space debris it creates.

> Space junk can be valuable. Researchers estimate that the recyclable material is worth billions or even trillions of dollars.

Let's Clean Up This Mess!

Like Earth before it, we have made space a garbage dump. But cluttered orbits threaten spacecraft, astronauts, and even people on Earth. As we continue to look to our future among the stars, we must also look for ways to solve space junk problems before they get worse.

We're tracking tiny debris, reusing rockets, building smarter spacecraft, and even developing strategies to recycle in space. We may have made a mess in space, but now we're going to clean it up!

Engineers are designing a spacecraft called the Electro Dynamic Debris Eliminator. This solar-powered, remote-controlled vehicle would be equipped with a net to sweep up low-orbiting space junk.

Part of the Space Junk Solution!

As someone living on Earth, it may feel like there's not a lot you can do to help clean up space. But the sky's the limit when it comes to contributing to the effort!

NASA is always looking for good ideas from the public. If you have a great idea for how to prevent or clean up space junk, send it in to NASA. You might be a part of the space solution!

Visit space centers and space museums to learn more about space junk and get some ideas for how to clean it up.

At your school's next science fair, do a presentation on space debris. Create a plan and model for a spacecraft that could collect and dispose of space junk.

If you are interested in space, start reading up on **aerospace** technology and engineering. Some day, you may become the inventor of the next mind-blowing space machine!

Educate your classmates, teachers, and family about space junk. Help them understand and get them involved in the effort to clean up space.

29

Glossary

aerospace the science of jet flight and space travel

astronauts people who travel into space

atmosphere layers of gases that surround Earth

debris the remains of something broken down or destroyed

discarded removed unwanted or useless pieces of something

lasers devices that create a very strong and narrow beam of light energy

maneuvered moved into place

obstacles things that block a path

orbit the circular path something travels around a star or planet; to move in this way is called orbiting

populated filled with many people living in a place

probes uncrewed spacecraft that are sent into space in order to send back photos and information

radar an instrument that uses radio waves to locate and measure distant objects

refurbished fixed or freshened up to work properly

satellites space machines that travel around Earth and gather information

vaporize to make vanish or destroy completely

Read More

Loh-Hagan, Virginia. *Space Junk (Weird Space Science: The Breakdown).* Ann Arbor, MI: 45th Parallel Press, 2025.

Markovics, Joyce. *Space Junk (Tech Bytes: Exploring Space).* Chicago: Norwood House Press, 2023.

Martin, Claudia. *Space Exploration (Space Revealed).* Minneapolis: Bearport Publishing, 2025.

Washburne, Sophie. *Satellites and Space Probes (The Inside Guide: Space Science).* Buffalo, NY: Cavendish Square, 2023.

Learn More Online

1. Go to **FactSurfer.com** or scan the QR code below.
2. Enter "**Decreasing Space Junk**" into the search box.
3. Click on the cover of this book to see a list of websites.

Index

astronauts 8, 15, 26
Astroscale 22
collisions 4, 12, 14, 18, 20–21
debris 5, 8, 10–12, 15–16, 18, 20–22, 24, 26, 29
end-of-life-services-by-Astroscale (ELSA) 22–23
European Space Agency (ESA) 22, 24
Falcon 9 18–19
fuel 9, 18, 24
International Space Station (ISS) 4, 15–16, 21
lasers 20–21
launch 6, 18–19
NASA 16, 29
ocean 10–11, 22

orbit 6, 8, 10, 12, 14, 18, 21–22, 24, 26
Orbital Debris Program (ODP) 16
radar 16–17
recycle 24, 26
reusable 18–19, 24, 26
rockets 4, 6, 8, 18–19, 24, 26
satellites 4–8, 10, 12, 14–16, 21–22, 24
spacecraft 6, 12, 16, 18, 22, 24, 26, 29
Space Systems Operations Research Laboratory (SSORL) 20–21
SpaceX 18–19
track 16, 26

About the Author

Raymond Bergin is a writer who lives in New Jersey and Massachusetts. One of his most memorable family vacations was a trip to the Kennedy Space Center in Cape Canaveral, Florida. To this day, he loves reading about the latest developments in space technology.